Whales

Tracy C. Read

FIREFLY BOOKS

A Firefly Book

Published by Firefly Books Ltd. 2017
Copyright © 2017 Firefly Books Ltd.
Text copyright © 2017 Tracy C. Read

For Audrey and Isaac, the next generation's shepherds of the sea.

First printing

Publisher Cataloging-in-Publication Data (U.S.)
Names: Read, Tracy C., author.
Title: Exploring the World of Whales / Tracy C. Read.
Description: Richmond Hill, Ontario, Canada : Firefly Books, 2017. | Series: Exploring the world of --- | Includes index. | Summary: "Up-close images and fascinating facts about whales" – Provided by publisher.
Identifiers: ISBN 978-1-77085-948-7 (hardcover) | 978-1-77085-949-4 (paperback)
Subjects: LCSH: Whales – Juvenile literature.
Classification: LCC QL737.C4R433 | DDC 599.5 – dc23

Library and Archives Canada Cataloguing in Publication
Read, Tracy C., author
    Exploring the world of whales / Tracy C. Read.
Includes index.
ISBN 978-1-77085-948-7 (hardcover).--ISBN 978-1-77085-949-4 (softcover)
    1. Whales--Juvenile literature. I. Title.
QL737.C4R4 2017   j599.5   C2017-902465-5

Published in the United States by
Firefly Books (U.S.) Inc.
P.O. Box 1338, Ellicott Station, Buffalo, New York 14205

Published in Canada by
Firefly Books Ltd.
50 Staples Avenue, Unit 1, Richmond Hill, Ontario L4B 0A7

Cover and interior design: Janice McLean/Bookmakers Press Inc.

Printed in China

Canada ◆ We acknowledge the financial support of the Government of Canada.

Front cover:
© Yann Hubert/Shutterstock

Back cover:
© Willyam Bradberry/Shutterstock

Back cover, inset, left:
© Mavenvision/Shutterstock

Back cover, inset, right top:
© Ken C Moore/Shutterstock

Back cover, inset, right bottom:
© Tory Kallman/Shutterstock

CONTENTS

ONE OF A KIND

The underside of a humpback's tail, below left, is unique to each whale. Photo identification creates a record that allows researchers to share information about sightings. Below middle and right: Three adult belugas swim in arctic waters; a closer look at the gray whale's short, coarse baleen plates.

MEET THE WHALES

A blast of spray in the distance, the slap of a tail fluke against the waves, the explosive sound and sight of a massive whale bursting from the ocean—spotting a whale in the wild is one of nature's most thrilling experiences.

With their typically sturdy, torpedo-shaped bodies, outfitted with insulating blubber, flippers, blowholes, tail flukes and fins, whales come in many sizes and forms. The ancient Greek philosopher and scientist Aristotle, one of the first serious whale watchers, recognized that there are two groups of whales: baleen and toothed. He also understood that whales are lung-breathing, warm-blooded mammals and not big, cold-blooded fish like the shark.

Humans have spent centuries killing whales for meat and oil, but today, we have learned to value them for their intelligence, diversity and wide-ranging behaviors. Some wander the world ocean; some make lengthy annual migrations to reproduce in warm waters; and some stay close to home.

Researchers continue to gather insights into the daily lives of the roughly 90 species of whale, dolphin and porpoise that live all over the planet. In this book, we'll introduce the baleen whales and some of the larger toothed whales, including the killer whale. Let's learn more about how these fascinating marine mammals have adapted to their chilly, challenging lives in the ocean.

4

WILD BLUE YONDER The sleek rorquals, including the blue, fin, sei, humpback and Bryde's whale, are the largest family of baleen whales. At roughly 95 feet (29 m) long, the blue whale, seen here, is the biggest animal ever to have lived on Earth, but the fin whale, at up to 88½ feet (27 m) is a close second. With long, pointed flippers and a tiny dorsal fin, the blue whale has a "splash guard" around its two blowholes. Its back is a dappled blue and light gray color, and these patterns help researchers identify individuals. Note the pleats running from its throat to its navel—these expand to allow the blue whale to take in huge mouthfuls of water and krill, its favorite food.

ANATOMY LESSON

When the land-dwelling ancestors of whales opted for a life in the sea some 50 million years ago, their bodies underwent a gradual but radical transformation. Their hind legs disappeared, forelimbs became paddlelike flippers, and their nostrils migrated to the top of the head. Most, but not all, developed a dorsal fin on their back.

Smooth skin and a thick layer of blubber that insulates the internal organs replaced heat-trapping fur. Blubber is also a protective barrier against attacks from predators such as killer whales and sharks. The bowhead whale lives only in arctic and subarctic waters and fights the cold with a one-inch (2.5 cm) layer of skin over blubber that is almost a foot (30 cm) thick.

Eventually, whales split into two suborders. Baleen whales feed by filtering tiny organisms and fish through baleen plates that hang from their upper jaw. Using echolocation, toothed whales send out sound waves that bounce back, allowing them to locate and pursue their prey.

Whales also became skilled swimmers and divers. With a muscular tail, known as flukes, and powerful flippers that occur in a variety of shapes and sizes, they are able to steer and navigate with great skill. To dive deep, they shut down organ function, collapse their lungs, lower their heart rate and rely on stored oxygen in their blood and muscles.

BLOCKHEAD

A close relative of the right whales, the arctic-dwelling bowhead whale is a baleen whale. It has an arched upper jaw, a large bulge around its blowholes and a big head, which it uses to break through two-foot-thick (60 cm) ice. The up to 65½-foot-long (20 m) bowhead outlives all other whales, easily over 100 years. Researchers wonder whether the bowhead's long life has something to do with its frigid habitat.

THE LIFE AQUATIC

One of the toothed whales, the killer whale, top, flashes its toothy grin. At up to 16 feet (5 m) long, the humpback whale's flippers, middle, are the largest appendage in nature. Bottom, the V-shaped burst of vapor from a gray whale distinguishes it as a baleen whale.

Eyes
Located on the sides of its head, whale eyes have upper and lower eyelids that open and close. Special glands release lubricants to flush away impurities.

Blowholes
Baleen whales, like this humpback, have two blowholes; toothed whales have one.

Upper and lower jaws
In baleen whales, baleen plates hang from the upper jaw like teeth from a comb. Toothed whales have varying numbers of teeth that come in all shapes and sizes. Some are used for snatching up prey; others are just for show.

Ventral pleats
Gulp-feeding baleen whales, such as the humpback, blue, fin, sei and minke, have abdominal pleats that expand to take in huge amounts of water and small fish.

Tongue
All whales have a tongue. Baleen whales use theirs to force out seawater and to gather the tiny prey that attaches to its baleen plates.

Tubercles and vibrissae
The humpback's body and flippers feature highly sensitive fist-sized bumps, or tubercles, that are actually hair follicles. Baleen whales have whiskerlike hairs called vibrissae around their mouth and head.

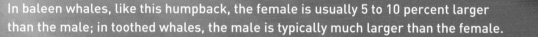

In baleen whales, like this humpback, the female is usually 5 to 10 percent larger than the male; in toothed whales, the male is typically much larger than the female.

Dorsal fin
Not all whales have a dorsal fin. Some fins are just a tiny knob or ridge; others are more robust. At close to 6 feet (1.8 m), the killer whale's is the tallest.

Speed demon
The fin whale may be the fastest of the large baleen whales, reaching speeds as high as 23 miles per hour (37 km/h).

Flukes
The boneless tail of a whale is all muscle. It is anchored to the whale's large spine.

Flippers
Whale flippers, or pectoral fins, come in various sizes and shapes, from slim and pointed to round and squarish. The surface area is supported by internal fingerlike bones.

Mammary glands
Female whales feed their calves underwater with two mammary glands located on the lower belly.

Humpback stats
Reaching a length of up to 55 feet 9 inches (17 m), a humpback weighs at least 88,000 pounds (40,000 kg). It has 14 to 35 ventral pleats that run from its throat to its navel.

NATURAL TALENTS

How do whales make use of the five senses—smell, taste, sight, touch and hearing—to navigate their vast liquid world?

Finding fuel for its big body is one of a whale's primary tasks, but is a whale able to sniff out a potential dinner beneath the sea? Although it takes in and releases oxygenated air through a blowhole, a whale can't breathe—or smell—underwater. When they come up for air, baleen whales may be able to pick up the fishy smell of a nearby mass of krill—traces of an olfactory organ have been found in their nasal tissue—but in toothed whales, there is no such evidence.

Whales gulp prey from a broth of salty water, and most are not overly picky eaters. Neither baleen whales nor toothed whales have well-developed taste buds and salivary glands. Some toothed whales may have evolved sensory organs that stand in for taste buds, but whether that affects their menu selection is still unclear.

Scientists have concluded that a whale is farsighted underwater and nearsighted on the surface. Reflective linings in the eyeball increase its ability to see prey in the dim underwater light, but the placement of its oval-shaped eyes on the sides of its head make depth perception impossible.

Whales experience touch through their skin, which is rich with nerves and blood vessels. They are most sensitive around the head, flippers, belly and genital area and

THERE'S OIL IN THEM THAR HEADS!

At up to 63 feet (19 m) long, the male sperm whale is the larges toothed whale. His huge, square he conceals the biggest brain of any mammal. It also contains a spermac organ filled with waxy fluid, which m this whale attractive to whalers. We now know this organ performs vital role in the production of the clicking sounds the sperm whale us in echolocation and communicatior

communicate through touch while playing, mating or rubbing against one another, especially mothers and calves. Whales may also communicate through tail and flipper slapping at the surface and breaching.

Thick whale ear bones insulate the inner ear from vibrations, and for all whales, hearing and the ability to produce sound are a critical part of how they connect with their world. The low-frequency moans and songs of the blue, fin, bowhead and minke whales and the complex symphonies of the humpbacks are messages that can be heard by whales hundreds of miles away. In a process called echolocation, the toothed whales send out razor-sharp clicks by moving air between air spaces in their head. Once they encounter a mass, these sounds bounce back to the whale's lower jaw. From here, vital information about prey, nearby animals and the seafloor is conducted through the bone to the brain.

HIGH PROFILE

A gray whale, top, pokes its head out of the water in a behavior known as spyhopping. It may be trying to decipher its location via the sound of the waves. Bottom: The only whale to grow a tusklike tooth, the narwhal plies the icy waters above the Arctic Circle, as does the beluga calf, facing page.

SMELL
Toothed whales like this beluga don't have a sense of smell. Baleen whales may be able to detect the strong scent of krill at the surface.

TOUCH
A whale experiences touch, cold, hot, pain and vibration through its skin. Most whales enjoy physical touching, especially mothers and their calves.

HEARING
Toothed whales rely on echolocation to pick up sounds. Baleen whale ear bones are built for hearing underwater.

SIGHT
Enlarged pupils let in more light, giving whales average vision in the dark ocean water. Above water, their eyesight is not as good.

TASTE
A big whale in search of a meal doesn't worry about flavor, but it may take into account a prey's size and scaliness and how easy it is to catch.

BRIEF ENCOUNTERS

Having a family is a major investment for a large mammal living in a vast ocean, especially when a newborn calf is roughly one-third its mother's size, as are baleen calves, or half her size, as are the calves of most toothed whales. At up to 26 feet (8 m) long, the blue whale's calf is the largest offspring on Earth. Baleen and toothed whales differ widely in their habitats and behaviors, but most give birth to a single calf every few years, taking some much-needed recovery time in between.

The blue-green waters off Patagonia, Argentina, churn and foam as the stocky male southern right whales gather. Some show off their vigor with an explosive breach from the water, and the air echoes with a blast as loud as a cannon shot. The right whales' hallmark head callosities and white belly markings glint in the sun.

These males have arrived to mate with a solitary female, and each wants a chance to father the next generation. As their robust bodies turn and tumble, the female may roll on her back to delay the inevitable. Eventually, she rolls over again and is belly to belly with the nearest male. Although all males—sometimes as many as 20—have a brief encounter with the lone female, only one, usually the last to mate, will be the father. This courtship ritual may go on for hours or days. Once it's over, the males head off.

SKIRMISH AT SEA
A surface-active group of male southern right whales attempt to mate with a female, above. Right whale individuals can be recognized by the rough skin patches, or callosities, that draw whale lice, as well as white patches on their bellies, top.

THE 'RIGHT' WHALE Hunted by whalers to near extinction because they are slow-moving and float when dead, right whales are considered endangered today. The Southern Hemisphere's southern right whale, seen here bursting from the water, or breaching, is a member of the healthiest of the three right whale species. The others are the North Atlantic right whale and the North Pacific right whale.

TOGETHER FOREVER

This young killer whale, or orca, is surrounded by its elders. The largest dolphin, an orca can reach lengths of up to 32 feet (9.8 m). Led by the oldest female, killer whales travel and hunt together in stable communities called pods. Breeding happens outside the pod.

NURSERY SCHOOL

Sperm whales may live to the age of 70 years or more. Male sperm whales roam the world ocean, but the much smaller females form long-term groups in warm and temperate waters with some 10 to 15 mothers and calves. Staying together, the females are able to defend their young against attacks by predators such as the killer whale.

A year or so later, the female gives birth to a calf.

Among the solitary baleen whales, the male humpbacks likewise compete for the female, although their approach can be more aggressive and some-times even violent. Gray whales have been witnessed rolling and rubbing together as a courtship ritual, with the male using his fins to help put the female into position. Males play no other part in family life, while most female baleen whales spend a year or so with their one calf, schooling it in the skills it will need to survive, before separating.

Generally, toothed whales are more social than baleen whales,

HUMPBACK BALLET

Born underwater, the humpback whale calf—seen here with its mother—is pushed to the surface for its first breath, then nursed on fat-rich milk for six months or so. The mother and calf are in constant contact over the first year, migrating together as the calf learns the skills needed to fend for itself.

and individuals may form ongoing relationships, traveling in groups of varying sizes. An adult male sperm whale may travel on his own, but he often forges a protective association with a nursery group of 10 or more adult females and their calves. This gives the male access to a harem of breeding partners. For the females, the group is a built-in child-care service. Several adult females guard the calves at the surface while one mother dives for dinner, often a deep-sea squid. Together, sperm whale mothers aggressively defend their young by forming a protective circle around a threatened calf.

Killer whales, which live in oceans all over the world, are the toothed whales with the most elaborate community structure. A female calf stays at her mother's side for 15 years before leaving to start her own family unit, but all offspring remain part of the original pod. Male calves are with their mothers for their entire lives—as long as 50 years. For the killer whale, mother always knows best.

DINNER RUSH

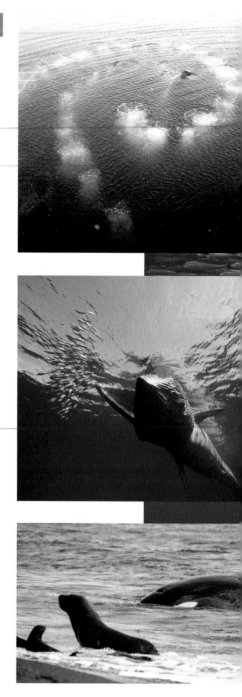

The huge, gaping mouth of a baleen whale in the midst of feeding instantly reveals the defining difference between baleen whales and toothed whales.

To capture a meal, a baleen whale opens its mouth wide and scoops up enormous quantities of water and small fish or tiny crustaceans known as krill. Plates of keratin (our fingernails are made from the same material) hang from its upper jaw, and these act like a sieve, holding the prey captive while the seawater filters out. The bowhead whale's up to 17-foot-long (5 m) baleen is the longest of any whale's, while the short, coarse baleen of the gray whale might be under 12 inches (30 cm) long. These stubby plates are well suited

for one of the gray whale's preferred eating strategies in shallow waters—using suction to sweep up food and water (as well as sediment) from the ocean floor.

Many (though not all) baleen whales also possess varying numbers of ventral pleats that expand, parachute-style, as the whale takes water and prey on board in a method known as lunge feeding. Cruising near a cluster of prey, the whale suddenly shifts into high gear, mouth agape. A coastal-feeding blue whale might take in 1,100 pounds (500 kg) of krill in a single lunge, easily replenishing the energy it spends capturing the up to 8,000 pounds (3,630 kg) of food it needs each day.

The big-headed right whales

CATCH OF THE DAY

Humpback whales, left, team up to blow a series of bubble nets to trap their prey. Middle: Ventral pleats expanded, a Bryde's whale turns on its side to scoop up a mass of little fish and seawater. A killer whale, bottom, makes its move on a mother seal and her pup.

BRYDE'S BAITBALL

A denizen of tropical and subtropical waters, a Bryde's whale cruises under a humongous baitball of mackerel just before deploying a lightning-fast lunge (see middle photo, facing page), gulping vast amounts of water and fish.

WHAT'S ON THE MENU?

Filter-feeding baleen whales consume enormous quantities of invertebrates, zooplankton, copepods, krill and small schooling fish. The toothed whales go after cod, salmon, mackerel and squid, as well as smaller prey. Some killer whale communities stick to a menu of fish; some have a taste for other marine mammals, such as seals and whales.

and the bowhead do without ventral pleats, opening their dramatically arched jaws to reveal a cavernous mouth as they skim feed microscopic copepods on the ocean's surface. Most of the baleen whales spend close to half a year feeding in the cold, food-rich northern waters, storing energy in their blubber before they migrate to warmer breeding grounds.

Toothed whales use their teeth to grasp and sometimes tear apart their catch. The beluga and narwhal fish for salmon and cod in arctic waters, using suction to take in prey. The deepest-diving toothed whales, the Cuvier's beaked and the sperm whale, can reach depths of 9,800 feet (3,000 m) to grab deep-sea squid.

Like the sperm whale, the killer whale makes its living all over the world. Killer whales may team up to knock a seal from an ice floe or to pursue a gray whale calf or shark, enjoying a hard-won family dinner after the kill.

FEEDING FRENZY

A group of humpback whales takes advantage of a prey-rich patch in the ocean, opening wide to show off their gigantic tongues and baleen plates. One of the few baleen whales that feed cooperatively, the humpback likes krill and many species of small schooling fish, including herring and sardines.

PERILS AT SEA

Targeted by whalers for their meat and oil, the great whales were brought close to extinction by the mid-20th century. Responding to passionate lobbying by conservationists, the International Whaling Commission announced a moratorium on commercial whaling in 1986. Some whale populations have since recovered, but through the rogue actions of Norway, Iceland and Japan, the slaughter continues.

Humans play a central role in jeopardizing whale recovery in a host of other ways. At the top of the list is pollution. We've treated the world ocean as a dumping ground for many decades. Pesticides, herbicides, fertilizers, detergents and sewage go untreated into the sea, eventually spawning algal bloom that robs the water of oxygen.

Today, there are some 400 dead zones in the world ocean where marine life is an impossibility.

In addition to liquid waste, there is solid waste. Plastic is the chief offender. It's estimated that there are 5.25 trillion pieces of plastic debris in the sea, and whale autopsies have shown that some of this debris finds its way into the marine food chain. Dubbed the Pacific trash vortex, a mass of plastic and garbage the size of Texas sits trapped by ocean currents in the North Pacific. The rest of the debris clogs river mouths and bays or is washed ashore.

While whales can become fatally entangled in discarded fishing nets, they are also affected by another kind of pollution: noise. Never have so many ships carried so much cargo to international ports. The noise from ship engines, in addition to that created by navy sonar and oil rigs, carries for miles through the ocean, potentially disrupting the migratory patterns of the big whales. And these ships often travel the same routes as the comparatively slow-moving whales, resulting in fatal or debilitating injuries through ship strikes.

The news isn't all bad, thanks

CETACEAN S.O.S.

Whales face a number of hazards in the world ocean, from liquid toxins and solid waste, left, and the impact of global warming to attacks by the marine-mammal-eating communities of killer whales, which think nothing of preying on another whale like this gray whale calf, bottom left. Bottom right: A researcher drops a hydrophone into the water to eavesdrop on whales.

MOVING TARGETS

One of 22 species of beaked whale, the highly social Baird's beaked whale continues to be hunted and killed by Japanese whalers. Since 2009, the Russian Cetacean Habitat Project has been studying Baird's beaked whales, killer whales and humpbacks in the Bering Sea.

to the dedicated, painstaking work of researchers and conservationists. Through photo identification, data-recording devices and biopsy darts, they are able to identify, track and count whales. With hydrophones, they can locate whales and record whale songs. All of this information is used to develop profiles of the planet's most intelligent marine mammals and to persuade governments that preserving safe habitats is essential. As a result, marine protected areas are being created all over the world.

Organizations like Whale and Dolphin Conservation fund international teams of researchers who are committed to preventing the future loss of whale species to the world. They all deserve our gratitude and support.

PHOTOS © BRANDON COLE
p. 4–5
p. 6 (top)
p. 12 (top)
p. 16 (left)
p. 17
p. 18 (middle)
p. 19
p. 21
p. 22 (bottom)

PHOTOS © SHUTTERSTOCK
p. 3 (middle) John Wollwerth
p. 3 (right) Jo Crebbin
p. 6 (middle) Martin Prochazkacz
p. 6 (bottom) Oksana Perkins
p. 8–9 jamesteohart
p. 10 Willyam Bradberry
p. 13 buchan
p. 15 Foto 4440
p. 16 (right): Monica Wieland Shields
p. 18 (bottom): Andrea Izzotti

p. 20 baitball: Leonardo Gonzalez
p. 20 fish: Miroslav Halama
p. 20 squid: Kondratuk Aleksei
p. 20 seal: Dmytro Pylypenko
p. 20 gray whale calf: Joost van Uffelen

p. 22 (top): Rich Carey

OTHER CONTRIBUTORS
p. 7 © Kelvin Aitken/VWPics/ Alamy Stock Photo
p. 14 (middle) © Mariano Sironi
pp. 12 (bottom), 14 (top), 18 (top) © Jean-Pierre Sylvestre
pp. 3 (left), 23 © Russian Cetacean Habitat Project (Whale and Dolphin Conservation)
p. 23 (bottom) © Far East Russia Orca Project (Whale and Dolphin Conservation)